infograp... HOW IT WORKS

LIFE ON EARTH

Editor: Liza Miller
Produced by Tall Tree Ltd
Editor: Jon Richards
Designer: Ed Simkins

ISBN: 978 0 7502 9969 5
10 9 8 7 6 5 4 3 2 1

MIX
Paper from
responsible sources
FSC® C104740
FSC
www.fsc.org

Wayland
An imprint of Hachette
Children's Group
Part of Hodder and Stoughton
Carmelite House
50 Victoria Embankment
London EC4Y 0DZ

An Hachette UK Company
www.hachette.co.uk
www.hachettechildrens.co.uk

Printed and bound in Dubai

CONTENTS

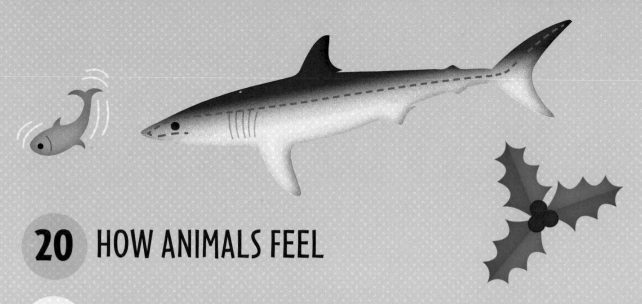

WORLD OF WONDER

Earth is home to a rich diversity of life, from microscopic plants to the blue whale. Living things have adapted to survive in nearly all parts of the globe, from the frozen polar wastes to the lush rainforests of the equator.

HOW MANY ARE THERE?

So far, scientists have named and catalogued about 1.5 million different types or species of living things. However, that is only a small amount of the life on earth today – estimates suggest that there may be as many as 14 million species in total.

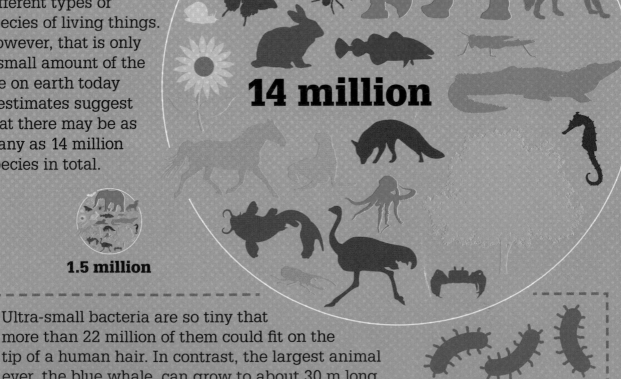

14 million

1.5 million

Ultra-small bacteria are so tiny that more than 22 million of them could fit on the tip of a human hair. In contrast, the largest animal ever, the blue whale, can grow to about 30 m long.

36% forest   **33% grassland**   **31% desert**

DIVERSE HABITATS

About 29 per cent of the earth's surface is covered with land; this is made up of three main types of habitat. The most extensive of these is forest, including tropical and coniferous forest. This is followed by grassland, such as the African savannah and the temperate grassland of the American prairie. Finally, the remainder is covered by desert, including the scorching deserts of Africa as well as the frozen wastes of the Arctic and Antarctic.

ALL CHANGE

Extinction, where species of living things disappear forever, plays a key part in the evolution of life on earth. Scientists have identified several key mass extinction events, when a lot of species died out at once. These include the Cretaceous-Tertiary extinction event about 66 million years ago, when the dinosaurs died out. The greatest extinction event ever was the Permian-Triassic, which saw almost all sea species disappear.

The Permian-Triassic extinction event occurred about 252 million years ago.

About 96 per cent of all marine species became extinct.

HOW PLANTS MAKE ENERGY

water

Plants have the amazing ability to turn sunlight into energy, which they need to grow. They do this using a special green chemical called chlorophyll. The conversion process is called photosynthesis.

1 ABSORBING

Plants absorb water from the ground through their roots. They also take in a gas called carbon dioxide, which is found in the air, through tiny holes in their leaves called stomata.

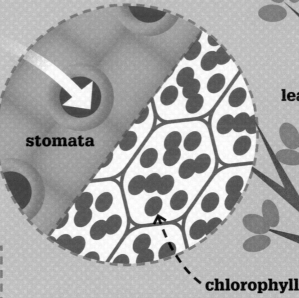

stomata

leaves

chlorophyll

Two fully grown trees release enough oxygen for a family of four people to breathe.

2 GREEN STUFF

Inside the cells that make up the leaves are tiny capsules called chloroplasts. These contain green chlorophyll.

roots

water

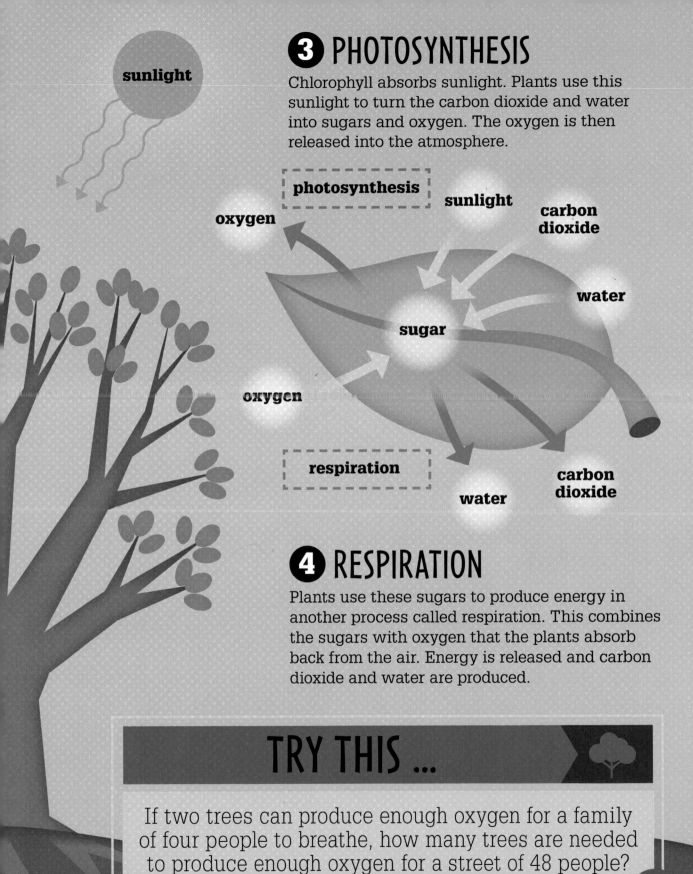

❸ PHOTOSYNTHESIS

Chlorophyll absorbs sunlight. Plants use this sunlight to turn the carbon dioxide and water into sugars and oxygen. The oxygen is then released into the atmosphere.

sunlight

photosynthesis

sunlight

carbon dioxide

oxygen

water

sugar

oxygen

respiration

carbon dioxide

water

❹ RESPIRATION

Plants use these sugars to produce energy in another process called respiration. This combines the sugars with oxygen that the plants absorb back from the air. Energy is released and carbon dioxide and water are produced.

TRY THIS ...

If two trees can produce enough oxygen for a family of four people to breathe, how many trees are needed to produce enough oxygen for a street of 48 people?

HOW PLANTS REPRODUCE

Plants use many methods to make more of themselves, known as reproduction. Many plants produce seeds by merging male and female cells. These seeds then grow into new plants.

1 CELLS

Flowers have male cells, contained in tiny pollen grains, and female cells, called ovules.

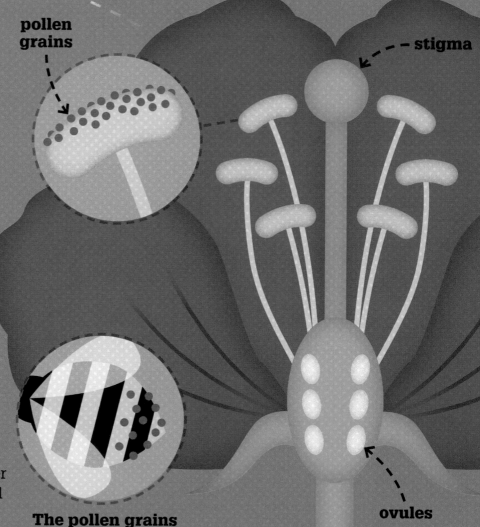

pollen grains

stigma

2 POLLEN

Pollen grains are carried to the stigma, a sticky part that is found at the centre of a flower. The pollen grains are carried either by the wind or by small animals, such as bees.

The pollen grains get stuck on a bee.

ovules

❸ MERGING

The pollen grains grow small tubes down the stigma until they reach an ovule. The male cells travel down this tube and merge with an ovule.

❹ SEEDS

The merged cells grow into a seed, which holds the developing plant, or embryo, and a food source called the endosperm.

embryo

endosperm

❺ DISPERSAL

The seed then leaves the parent plant using a number of methods. It can be eaten as part of fruit, blown away on the wind or carried away by water.

❻ GROWING

Once the seed has reached a suitable place and the conditions are right, it germinates or starts to grow.

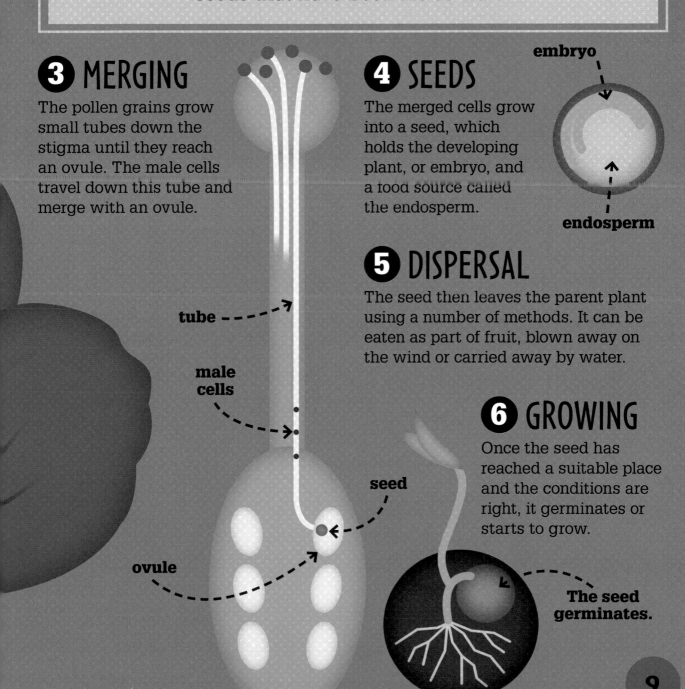

tube

male cells

seed

ovule

The seed germinates.

9

HOW ANIMALS HAVE BABIES

Most animals reproduce by merging cells from male and female parents. This is called sexual reproduction. Once the two cells have combined, they can develop in very different ways. Some animals will lay eggs that grow into young, while others give birth to live babies.

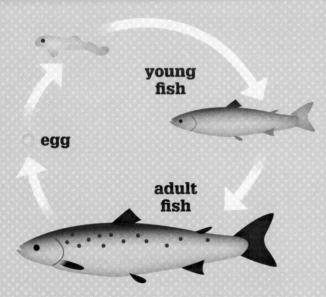

young fish

egg

adult fish

1 LIVING IN WATER

Animals that lay eggs in water, such as fish and frogs, usually produce soft eggs. Each egg contains the developing young as well as a small supply of food.

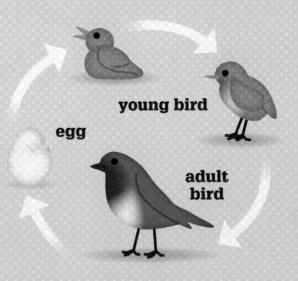

young bird

egg

adult bird

2 HATCHING FROM EGGS

Animals that lay eggs on land, such as snakes and birds, produce eggs with hard or leathery shells. These stop the eggs from drying out. When it's time to hatch, the baby animals often use a beak or a special egg tooth to break open their shell.

Monotremes are unusual mammals that lay eggs. This group includes platypuses and echidnas.

young dog

adult dog

❸ LIVE BIRTH

The babies of some animals develop inside the mother, in a part called the womb, where they are fed and protected. When they are born, they may be able to look after themselves, or they might need further protection by their parents.

The record for the largest dog litter belongs to a Neopolitan mastiff called Tia, who gave birth to 24 puppies in total.

❹ POUCHES

The young of some mammals, such as kangaroos, do not fully develop inside the mother. Instead, the tiny young crawl into a special pouch where they feed on the mother's milk and continue to develop.

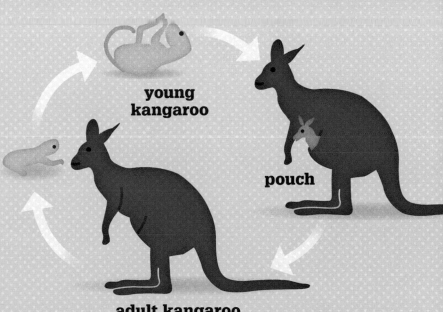

young kangaroo

pouch

adult kangaroo

TRY THIS ...

It is estimated that about five per cent of frogs survive from spawn to maturity. If a frog lays 300 eggs, how many will reach adulthood?

HOW PREDATORS HUNT

Predators are animals that hunt and eat other animals. Predators use different methods to catch their prey. These include hiding and waiting for unsuspecting prey to pass before leaping out to ambush it, or working together as a team to chase and catch food.

The stripes help to hide the tiger.

1 HIDING

Lone predators, such as tigers, rely on surprise to catch their prey. A tiger's fur has stripes, which help to hide it in the long grass and trees.

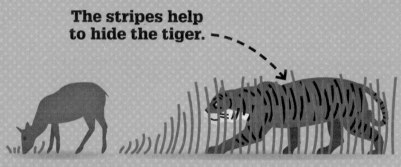

2 APPROACH

A hunting tiger will approach its prey so that it is downwind. This means any prey will not be able to smell the approaching tiger.

wind

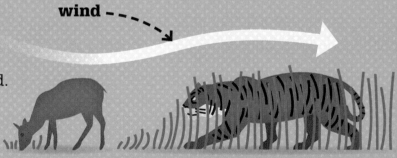

3 POUNCE

When the tiger is close enough, it will leap at the prey, using its speed and strength to bring the animal down and kill it.

❶ CHASE

Team predators work together to catch animals. A pack of wolves will start by chasing a herd of prey animals, such as moose.

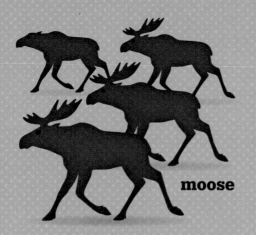

moose

leader

❷ TAKING TURNS

As the wolves chase the prey, they will take turns to lead the hunt. This helps the wolves to save energy during the chase.

❸ SEPARATING

The wolves will then separate out one of the prey animals. This is usually an old, young or sick animal.

young moose

❹ ATTACK

As the moose gets tired, the wolves jump on its back and bite the shoulders, side and neck. The moose loses blood and gets too tired to keep running. The wolves then rush in to make the kill.

TRY THIS ...

Think about how other predators hunt and catch their prey. Make a list of the tactics they use and what weapons they might have, such as claws or teeth.

13

HOW LIVING THINGS ADAPT

In order to survive, animals and plants need features that allow them to thrive in the local conditions, whether this is a warm, wet rainforest, freezing polar ice sheets or a harsh, dry desert.

Thick, double-layered fur and a layer of fat under the skin help to keep the body warm.

① COLD LIVING

Polar bears live on the ice sheets and islands of the Arctic. Their features allow them to survive freezing temperatures and to swim from one ice floe to another over great distances.

Fur on the paws helps to insulate polar bears against the ice and snow.

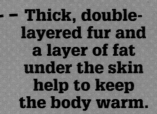

A streamlined body helps the shark to move through the water easily.

② UNDERWATER PREDATORS

Sharks are predators that are found in all of the earth's oceans. Their features allow them to move through the water easily as they hunt for prey.

A keen sense of smell can detect prey over great distances.

❸ LIFE ON THE PLAINS

Giraffes have adaptations that help them to live on the grasslands of Africa. A giraffe has a strong heart in order to pump blood all the way up its long neck.

The long neck allows it to reach high-up leaves that no other plant-eaters can reach.

A spotted pattern on its fur helps to hide the giraffe among trees.

The thick stem holds water reserves.

Sharp spines protect the plant from animals.

❹ DRY CONDITIONS

Cactuses have adaptations that help them to survive in dry deserts. Their features reduce water loss and stop animals from eating their leaves.

TRY THIS ...

Camels have features that allow them to survive in harsh, dry deserts. Can you make a list of the adaptations camels have and why they help them to survive in their habitat?

HOW ANIMALS SEE

Human eyes can see things in amazing detail and in a dazzling range of colours. But many animals have even better vision than we do. They can detect objects and patterns that are invisible to us.

1 COLLECTING

Eyes collect light and bend it to create a sharp image.

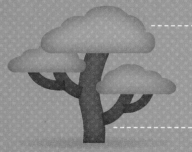

light

lens

pupil

iris

eyeball

Cats' eyes shine when you point a light at them because of a layer inside their eyes called the tapetum lucidum. This layer reflects light back into the eye, making cat vision very sensitive.

TRY THIS ...

Stand about 2 m from a friend and throw a tennis ball or bean bag between the two of you. It's easy to catch when you have both your eyes open. Now close one eye and try throwing and catching again. Do you find it easier or harder to do?

➋ CELLS

When light hits the back of the eye, it triggers chemical reactions inside special cells that line the inside of the eyeball.

image

← - - - - - cells

nerve signal

➌ SIGNALS

These reactions create nerve signals which travel to the brain. There, the signals are turned into a picture.

Humans see light that makes up what we call the visible spectrum – this contains all the colours of the rainbow. But some animals can see things that are invisible to us.

the visible spectrum - - ➚

Bees can see ultraviolet rays of light which are invisible to us. Some flowers use ultraviolet colouration to attract bees and guide them to where the pollen is.

visible light

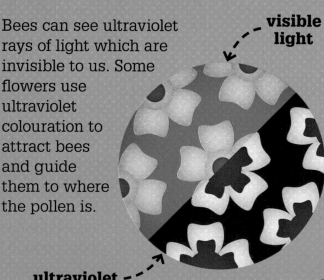

ultraviolet - - ➚

17

HOW ANIMALS SMELL

Animals use their sense of smell to detect scents in the world around them. This includes where something good to eat may be, whose territory they are in or a warning that a predator is creeping up on them. Snakes are particularly good at sniffing out prey.

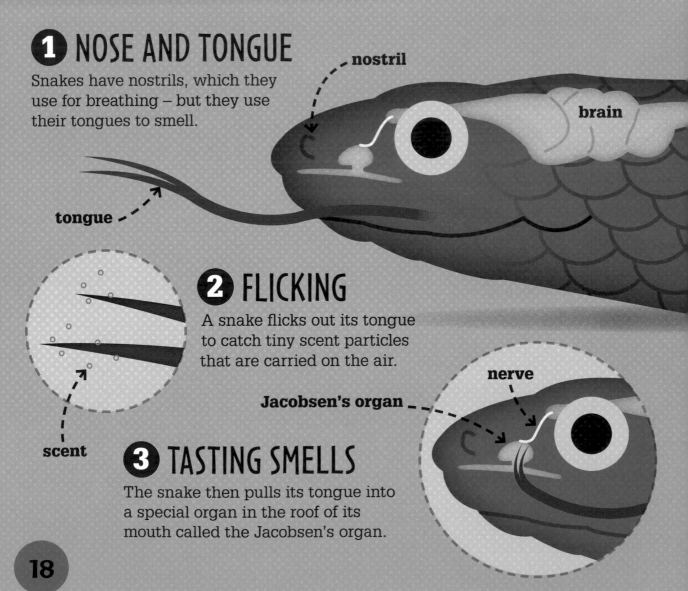

1 NOSE AND TONGUE

Snakes have nostrils, which they use for breathing – but they use their tongues to smell.

nostril

brain

tongue

2 FLICKING

A snake flicks out its tongue to catch tiny scent particles that are carried on the air.

scent

nerve

Jacobsen's organ

3 TASTING SMELLS

The snake then pulls its tongue into a special organ in the roof of its mouth called the Jacobsen's organ.

TRY THIS ...

Is your sense of smell as good as a snake's? Sit on a chair in the middle of a room and put on a blindfold. Then ask a friend to get something smelly (like a peeled orange or some cheese) and stand somewhere in the room. Can you use your sense of smell to detect where they are standing?

Sharks have a very good sense of smell. Some species of shark can detect one drop of blood or fish oil among 10 billion drops of water – that's the same as a single drop in an Olympic swimming pool!

❺ DIRECTION

Some scientists believe that snakes use their forked tongues to tell where a scent is coming from. More scent particles on one of the forks means that the scent's source is in that direction.

❹ SIGNALS

Here, the scent particles create nerve signals which travel to the snake's brain, where the smell is interpreted.

More scent is detected on the left.

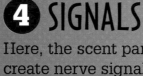

A rafflesia flower smells like rotting meat.

Some flowers produce a scent that smells like rotting meat. This attracts insects, which then carry the flowers' pollen off to other plants.

19

HOW
ANIMALS FEEL

Many animals have special senses which they use to detect the world around them. These senses help them track down prey or spot any predators trying to sneak up on them.

Vibrations pass into the skull.

1 VIBRATIONS

Snakes don't hear using ears on the outside of their heads as we do. Instead, vibrations made by sounds or by other animals moving about pass through a snake's skin and body to the inner ear, where the vibrations are changed into nerve signals and sent to the brain.

vibrations

2 SENSITIVE LINE

Sharks have a line of sensitive organs, known as the lateral line, running down the length of their bodies. These detect vibrations in the water, such as those caused by the thrashing about of wounded prey.

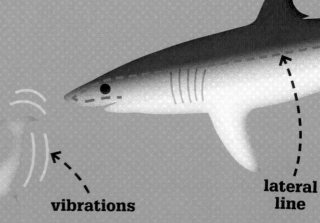

vibrations

lateral line

➌ SENSITIVE NOSE

In dark underground tunnels, the star-nosed mole uses the fleshy stalks on the end of its snout to detect vibrations caused by any approaching prey.

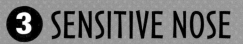

The stalks on the end of a star-nosed mole's snout contain 25,000 sensors.

➍ PLATYPUS BILL

All living animals produce tiny electrical signals in their muscles, even when they are still. A duck-billed platypus has about 40,000 tiny sensors in its bill. It sweeps its head around as it swims. When the sensors detect the electrical signals made by the prey's body, the platypus swoops in for its next meal.

electrical signals

bill

TRY THIS ...

Place your head on its side on a table and close your eyes. Ask a friend to tap on the table and see if you can detect the distance and direction of the taps, just like a snake.

HOW PLANTS PROTECT THEMSELVES

While some plants, such as fruit trees, want bits of themselves to be eaten, others go to great lengths to stop animals munching on them.

❶ PRICKLY STUFF

Many plants are covered with sharp points to stop animals eating them. These include the prickles on a cactus, a rose's sharp thorns and the pointed leaves on a holly bush.

sharp points

❷ CHEMICALS

Nettles are covered in tiny hollow hairs. These hairs contain chemicals which irritate an animal's skin if they brush up against it.

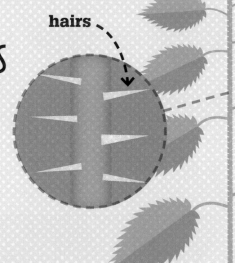

hairs

❸ POISONS

While some plants produce berries that can be eaten, others make poisonous berries to protect the seeds inside. In nature, bright colours are used to show that something may be dangerous, so many of these poisonous berries are brightly coloured.

④ TOUGH NUT

Coconut plants protect the juicy fruit inside with armour, which is made up of thick layers of fibres.

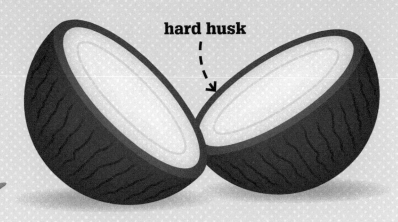

hard husk

⑤ CLOSING UP

Some plants close up if an animal brushes against them. This makes it harder for an animal to eat the leaves, and can also knock off any insects that are trying to feed.

hollow thorns

⑥ HOMES

Some plants produce special structures that make ideal homes for creatures that deter plant-eaters. For example, some acacia trees have hollow thorns where ants make their nests. These ants fight off plant-eating animals.

TRY THIS ...

On a walk through a park or the countryside, see if you can spot any plants with defences. These could include prickly thorns or leaves, tough bark or brightly coloured berries which could be poisonous – so don't touch!

HOW ANIMALS AVOID BEING EATEN

Animals have many adaptations to protect themselves from being spotted and caught by predators. These include living in protective groups with others, avoiding detection by having perfect camouflage or having a nasty sting.

❶ HIDING IN A CROWD

Zebras have bright black and white stripes, which makes them easy to spot. However, when hundreds of zebras are rushing about, the stripes can confuse a predator.

leaf insect

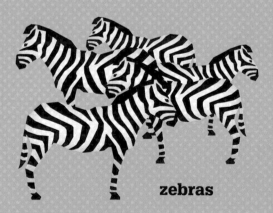

zebras

❸ LEAVES

A leaf insect has legs and body parts that are shaped to look like leaves. Some of these insects even rock back and forth so that they look like leaves waving in the wind.

❷ WRIGGLING TAIL

Other animals avoid being eaten by having a good escape plan. Some lizards shed their tails if they are attacked. The tail wriggles about, distracting the predator while the lizard escapes.

‑ ‑ **tail**

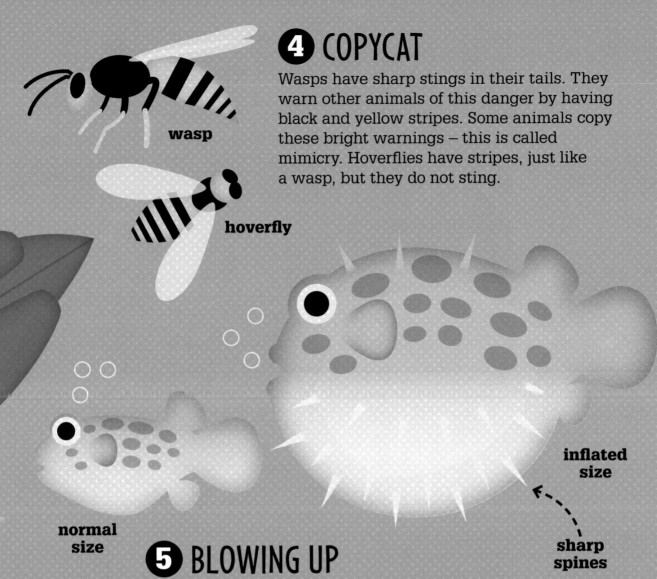

❹ COPYCAT

Wasps have sharp stings in their tails. They warn other animals of this danger by having black and yellow stripes. Some animals copy these bright warnings – this is called mimicry. Hoverflies have stripes, just like a wasp, but they do not sting.

wasp

hoverfly

inflated size

sharp spines

normal size

❺ BLOWING UP

Puffer fish have an amazing defence against predators. When predators are nearby, they inflate themselves into huge prickle-covered balls!

TRY THIS ...

Design your own camouflage patterns to hide in a sandy desert environment and in a leafy rainforest. Think about the environments you need to hide in. Which colours and shapes will help to camouflage you?

HOW ANIMALS SURVIVE A SHORTAGE

Many animals live in parts of the world where food and water are scarce or conditions are very harsh. These animals have adapted to survive such periods of shortage.

1 MIGRATION

Many animals move from place to place in search of food. This movement is called migration, and it can happen over thousands of kilometres or just a short distance. Krill move up and down in the ocean just a few metres every day to feed off tiny plankton.

krill

plankton

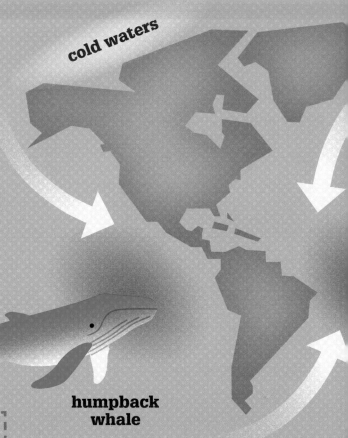

cold waters

humpback whale

Some plants go dormant when water is scarce or conditions aren't good for growing. One lotus seed found on a dried-up lake bed in China germinated after having been dormant for 1,300 years!

2 LONG SWIM

Humpback whales swim thousands of kilometres every year, from the poles where they feed on krill during the summer to warmer waters where they breed and raise their young.

1 HIBERNATION

Some creatures slow their bodies down during winter so that they use less energy. This is called hibernation. Before they start to hibernate, some animals eat lots of food to build up their fat stores so they can survive the cold months.

Bears can lose up to one-third of their body weight during hibernation.

While they are hibernating, some bears do not eat or drink at all, relying instead on fats and liquids stored in their bodies.

cold waters

warm waters

cold waters

2 SLOW DOWN

Hibernating animals slow down their body rate, or metabolism. A bear can slow its metabolic rate by 50 to 60 per cent.

TRY THIS ...

Help some animals to survive the winter by putting out insect 'hotels' for bugs to hibernate in, and by scattering bird food when it gets cold.

HOW LIVING THINGS ARE RECYCLED

All living things form part of a cycle of nutrients and chemicals, and this cycle does not stop when something dies. Instead, a dead body is recycled by tiny organisms, which release the chemicals stored in the body back into the environment.

CO_2

CO_2

❶ THE CARBON CYCLE

Carbon is an element that moves through plants, animals, earth and the air in a cycle. Our bodies contain lots of carbon and we also release carbon dioxide into the atmosphere when we breathe out. The carbon cycle includes photosynthesis when plants use carbon dioxide to produce sugars and oxygen, and respiration when all living things produce energy and give off carbon dioxide.

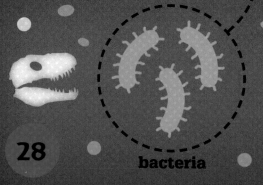

❷ DECOMPOSE

When a living thing dies, bacteria start to decompose the body using enzymes. The process releases carbon from the body into the air as carbon dioxide.

bacteria

TRY THIS ...

Put a piece of fruit in a bowl and leave it on a warm window ledge (ask an adult before you do this as things may get smelly). Watch the fruit over a number of days and study how it starts to rot and break down as tiny organisms recycle its nutrients.

In the last 150 years, the burning of fossil fuels, such as coal, natural gas and oil, has released nearly 250 billion tonnes of carbon into the air.

CO_2

❹ BURNING FUEL

When the fuel is burned, it releases the carbon it holds into the atmosphere.

- - oil and gas

❸ FOSSIL FUELS

In some conditions, the dead body may not decompose. Instead, it may be turned into a fossil fuel, which can be burned in the future.

GLOSSARY

AMBUSH
To attack something by surprise.

ATMOSPHERE
The layer of gases that surrounds a planet.

BACTERIA
Tiny forms of life that are made up of just one cell.

CAMOUFLAGE
Something that hides an object against its background, such as the stripes on a tiger or the shape of a leaf insect.

CELLS
The basic units that make up living organisms. They contain genetic material which tells the cells how to grow and behave.

CHEMICAL REACTION
A process that changes the chemical structure of a substance or produces heat.

CONIFEROUS
A type of tree that has small, needle-like leaves which last all-year round.

DECOMPOSE
When something breaks down into simpler substances.

DIVERSITY
A measure of the range of different things that are found in an area. Diversity can relate to the number and range of animal and plant species that live in a region.

DORMANT
When a plant or animal enters a sleep-like state.

ENZYMES
Substances that help or speed up chemical reactions.

EQUATOR
The imaginary line which runs around Earth at its widest part.

GERMINATE
When a seed starts to grow.

ICE FLOE
A piece of free-floating ice.

ICE SHEET
A thick layer of ice that covers a large area of land.

INNER EAR
The part of the ear that holds the organs that change sounds into nerve signals.

INSULATE
To reduce the flow of heat energy from an object, keeping it either cool or warm.

KRILL
Tiny shrimp-like animals.

LATERAL
Something that runs along the sides of a body.

MAMMALS
A type of animal that has a backbone, is warm-blooded and produces milk to feed its young.

MARINE
Something that is found in the seas and oceans.

METABOLIC RATE
The rate at which a living organism operates and uses energy.

MICROSCOPIC
Something that is too small to see with the naked eye.

NUTRIENTS
A useful substance which a living organism can absorb to survive and grow.

PARTICLES
Very small pieces of something.

PLANKTON
Tiny plants and animals that live close to the ocean's surface.

POLLEN
Tiny grains that contain the male sex cells of plants.

PRAIRIE
The large area of grassland that lies in the middle of the North American continent.

PREDATOR
An animal that hunts and kills other animals for food.

PREY
An animal that is eaten by a predator.

SAVANNAH
The large area of grassland that lies in the middle of Africa.

SPAWN
The large amount of eggs laid by a fish or amphibian.

SPECIES
A group of living organisms that are very similar to each other and can give birth to offspring which can also have babies.

TEMPERATE
Something that is found in the regions lying halfway between the Equator and the poles.

ULTRAVIOLET
A type of light that humans cannot see.

WOMB
Also called the uterus, this is the organ inside most female mammals where young develop before birth.

ANSWERS ...

14-15 Among other adaptations, camels have large feet to stop them sinking in sand, can go for long periods without drinking water, store fat in their humps as an energy source and have long eyelashes to keep sand out of their eyes.

10-11 15 frogs will reach maturity.

6-7 You would need 24 trees to produce enough oxygen for 48 people.

INDEX

WEBSITES

www.ngkids.co.uk
Website by National Geographic that's packed with videos, facts and games on the natural world, and a whole lot more.

www.zsl.org/kids-zsl
Created by the Zoological Society of London, this website is full of games, activities and information about animals.

www.wildlifewatch.org.uk
The website of the junior branch of The Wildlife Trusts, this contains information, activities and blogs about plants and animals in the UK, as well as guides for teachers and group leaders.